BOOK WORMS

Step-by-Step Transformations

Turning Wheat into Bread

Amy Hayes

Cavendish Square
New York

Published in 2016 by Cavendish Square Publishing, LLC
243 5th Avenue, Suite 136, New York, NY 10016

Library of Congress Cataloging-in-Publication Data

Hayes, Amy, author.
Turning wheat into bread / Amy Hayes.
pages cm. — (Step-by-step transformations)
Includes index.
ISBN 978-1-50260-446-0 (hardcover) ISBN 978-1-50260-445-3 (paperback) ISBN 978-1-50260-447-7 (ebook)
1. Bread—Juvenile literature. 2. Wheat—Juvenile literature. I. Title.

TX769.H3935 2016
641.8'15—dc23

2014049224

Editorial Director: David McNamara
Copy Editor: Cynthia Roby
Art Director: Jeffrey Talbot
Designer: Alan Sliwinski
Senior Production Manager: Jennifer Ryder-Talbot
Production Editor: Renni Johnson
Photo Research by J8 Media

Photos by: smereka/Shutterstock.com, cover; Scorpp/Shutterstock.com, cover; Petar Chernaev/E+/Getty Images, 5; Rob Whitrow/Photolibrary/Getty Images, 7; avs/Shutterstock.com, 9; Janina Laszlo/STOCK4B/Getty Images, 11; gezzeg/Shutterstock.com, 13; Scott Indermaur/Photolibrary/Getty Images, 15; Mypurgtoryyears/iStockPhoto.com, 17; Tim Platt/Photolibrary/Getty Images, 19; Fabrice LEROUGE/ONOKY/Getty Images, 21.

Printed in the United States of America

Contents

Bread is made from wheat.

First, the wheat is **milled**, or crushed, into small pieces.

The milled wheat is called flour.

7

Next, water, **yeast**, and other **ingredients** are added to the flour.

They mix together to become dough.

9

After that, a **divider** cuts up the dough.

Then, the dough is rolled into balls.

Now the dough is sent to rest.

It sits for a few minutes.

13

Then, the dough goes into a pan and is put in a warm room.

The dough **rises**.

14

15

Now it is time to bake
the dough.

The dough goes into a
big oven.

17

Finally, the dough has been baked into bread.

19

We eat bread with lots of foods.

Bread tastes great!

21

New Words

divider (di-VY-der) A machine that breaks up dough into equal parts.

ingredients (in-GREE-dee-entz) Parts that mix together to make a certain thing.

milled (MILLED) To grind into flour, meal, or powder.

rises (RYZ-ez) When dough expands in a warm, closed space.

yeast (YEEST) An ingredient in bread that makes it rise.

Index

About the Author

Amy Hayes lives in the beautiful city of Buffalo, New York. She has written several books for children, including the Machines that Work and the Our Holidays series for Cavendish Square.

About BOOK WORMS

Bookworms help independent readers gain reading confidence through high-frequency words, simple sentences, and strong picture/text support. Each book explores a concept that helps children relate what they read to the world in which they live.